L♥VE®
IT TOGETHER !
Make a better future

CAROL-ANN MELTZER

Balboa Press books may be ordered through booksellers or by contacting:

Balboa Press
A Division of Hay House
1663 Liberty Drive
Bloomington, IN 47403
www.balboapress.com
1 (877) 407-4847

ISBN: 978-1-9822-3239-9 (sc)
ISBN: 978-1-9822-3240-5 (e)

Print information available on the last page.

Balboa Press rev. date: 09/20/2019

BALBOA
PRESS
A DIVISION OF HAY HOUSE

visit
www.loveittogether.com
for your
Pledge of Possibility!

Contents

LOVE IT TOGETHER

We're makin' a love bomb
Lovebomb
Everyone get some
We're makin' a love bomb
Sugar candy love machine
We are working in a team
Rainbow, music, rhythm and beat
Come to the place where the good
people meet
Do we stay?
Do we go?
Can you tell me, please
Cos I'm here waiting for you

This is the song
This is the tune
This is the melody
The symphony rocking the radio
Love it together
This is the sign
This is the ray
This is the gift that opens my every day
This is the light that brings in alright
And it makes everything a delicious delight

I love it together
Love it together
Love it together
Love it together

Even though across the world we're apart
We are all beating with one heart
The feeling is love
That's what we're made of

This is the course we don't need to force our way no longer
We are stronger than ever
Love it together

We're all in this together
It doesn't matter whatever you do
We're all in this together
Love it together

Life isn't just one thing
We don't know what the future's gonna bring
It doesn't matter whether we're birds of a feather
Love it together
Like the wind
You can't see
Know
Blow
Together
Love it together

Love it together
Love it together

5

THE BEST TIME IS NOW

The best time is now
You can wait till tomorrow
But it's never gonna come
If you're waiting for someone
To make your dreams come true
You got to do them now
Wow wow wow wow
The best time is now

Da da dum da dum
Da da dum da dum
Da da dum da dum
Da da dum da dum
Da da dum da dum

WHO CARES?

CHORUS:
Who cares?
Who cares about society
The city or their 'ome?
Are we alone?
Are we together?
Who cares?
Who cares?

How do you do?
And where do you go?
Does anyone bother?
Does anyone care to know?
Do you have any anxiety
Through the thick and thin?
We can only imagine where you've been

CHORUS:
Who cares?
Who cares about society
The city or their 'ome?
Are we alone?
Are we together?
Who cares?
Who cares?

Castles in the sky
Are you still high?
Does anyone bother?
Does anyone care to know?
Do you have any anxicty
Through the thick and thin?
We can only imagine where you've been

Playing the game
Are we the same?
Does anyone bother?
Does anyone care to know?
Do you have any anxiety
Through the thick and thin?
We can only imagine where you've been

BRIDGE:
Caring is sharing
Is it real or is it totally fake?
Make no mistake
Selfish is popular
It's popular today
Everybody wants their own way

CHORUS:
Who cares?
Who cares about society
The city or their home?
Are we alone? Are we together?
Who cares?
Who cares?

Keep putting one foot before the other
Walk with your sister and your brother
Keep pushing
Keep pushing on

Keep putting one foot before the other
Walk with your sister and your brother
Keep pushing
Keep pushing on

LANGUAGE OF LOVE

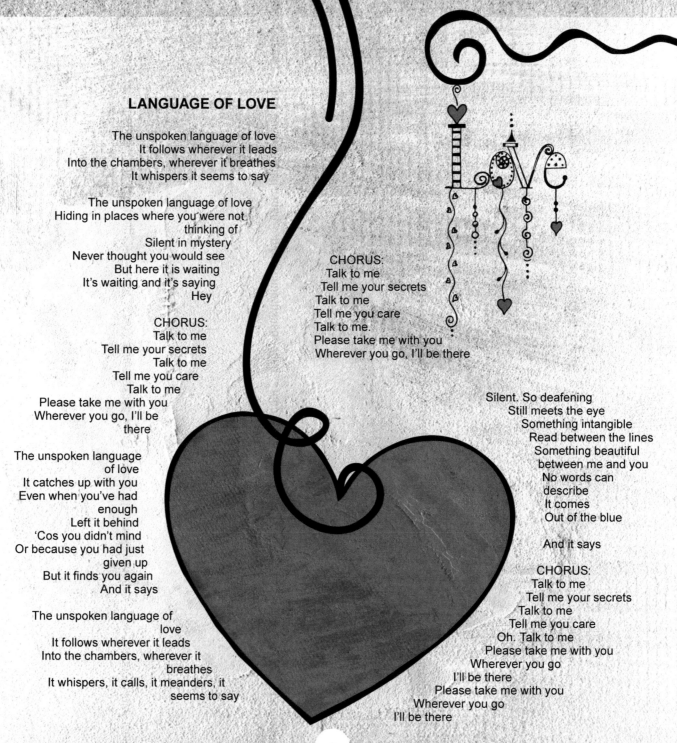

The unspoken language of love
It follows wherever it leads
Into the chambers, wherever it breathes
It whispers it seems to say

The unspoken language of love
Hiding in places where you were not
thinking of
Silent in mystery
Never thought you would see
But here it is waiting
It's waiting and it's saying
Hey

CHORUS:
Talk to me
Tell me your secrets
Talk to me
Tell me you care
Talk to me
Please take me with you
Wherever you go, I'll be
there

The unspoken language
of love
It catches up with you
Even when you've had
enough
Left it behind
'Cos you didn't mind
Or because you had just
given up
But it finds you again
And it says

The unspoken language of
love
It follows wherever it leads
Into the chambers, wherever it
breathes
It whispers, it calls, it meanders, it
seems to say

CHORUS:
Talk to me
Tell me your secrets
Talk to me
Tell me you care
Talk to me.
Please take me with you
Wherever you go, I'll be there

Silent. So deafening
Still meets the eye
Something intangible
Read between the lines
Something beautiful
between me and you
No words can
describe
It comes
Out of the blue

And it says

CHORUS:
Talk to me
Tell me your secrets
Talk to me
Tell me you care
Oh. Talk to me
Please take me with you
Wherever you go
I'll be there
Please take me with you
Wherever you go
I'll be there

BEAUTIFUL DAY

CHORUS:
Hey, Hey, Hey
It's a beautiful day
Hey, Hey, Yeh
It's a beautiful day
No matter what you say
It is a beautiful day
Keep the sunshine shining through

No matter where you are
No matter near or further away
I've come to say have a brilliant day
No matter what you do
Be good to you
Others will follow
Maybe we'll see a new tomorrow

Sometimes it doesn't take much to smile
Or to laugh once in a while
Sometimes the best things are free
That's why there's always you and me

CHORUS:
Hey, Hey, Hey
It's a beautiful day
Hey, Hey, Yeh
It's a beautiful day
No matter what you say
It is beautiful day
Keep the sunshine shining through

There is always room to change
The way we live from day to day
Learn from past mistakes
Sooner or later we will have to wake up
From the dreariness of just getting by

CHORUS:
Hey, Hey, Hey
It's a beautiful day
Hey, Hey, Yeh
It's a beautiful day
No matter what you say
It is a beautiful day
Keep the sunshine shining through
Keep the sunshine shining through
Keep the sunshine shining through

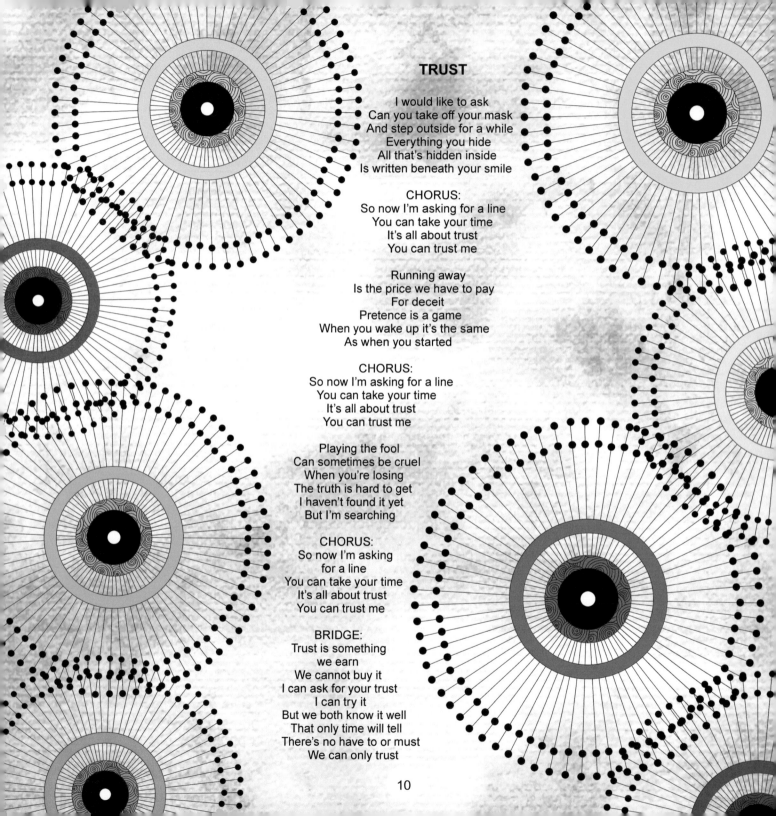

TRUST

I would like to ask
Can you take off your mask
And step outside for a while
Everything you hide
All that's hidden inside
Is written beneath your smile

CHORUS:
So now I'm asking for a line
You can take your time
It's all about trust
You can trust me

Running away
Is the price we have to pay
For deceit
Pretence is a game
When you wake up it's the same
As when you started

CHORUS:
So now I'm asking for a line
You can take your time
It's all about trust
You can trust me

Playing the fool
Can sometimes be cruel
When you're losing
The truth is hard to get
I haven't found it yet
But I'm searching

CHORUS:
So now I'm asking
for a line
You can take your time
It's all about trust
You can trust me

BRIDGE:
Trust is something
we earn
We cannot buy it
I can ask for your trust
I can try it
But we both know it well
That only time will tell
There's no have to or must
We can only trust

10

MUSIC

First you get the rhythm
Then you get the beat
You can feel vibrations
Through your feet
There ain't no substitute
This is the natural way
If you can energise
The magic will stay

Music is light
If we feel it right
Can you feel your emotions
Moving like the oceans
Music is a message
A message to the soul
Many mixed emotions
Come we're on a roll

CHORUS: (x2)
Let's make music
Let's make music
Music, Music, Music

Music is a magic
It sounds its magic wand
You can feel much better now
As you move beyond
Music is a spirit of the dancing tribe
You can touch intangible
If you feel the vibe
CHORUS: (x2)
Let's make music
Let's make music
Music, Music, Music

In the yin and the yang
And the big bang
Soaring on the hilltops of love
A sound sensation
Calls for meditation
It is down, around, below
And up above

CHORUS: (x2)
Let's make music
Let's make music
Music, Music, Music
Music
Yeh

WAR

Time takes its toll
Bankruptcy denies the doll
Poverty will lead to crime
Mass procrastination
In the era of a nation

Domestic arms race
Fear and pain
Shall we kill again and again
What's the use if we're heading for heaven
Why the AK47
Get your licence
Get your gun
Death penalty's been undone
So now you do as you feel free
Something tells me – this can't be

Testing tolerance
Mass incompetence
Begging for their daily bread
Close proximity
Mass anxiety
Everyone needs clothing and a roof over their heads

Now if everyone looked after themselves
No-one would have to look after anyone else
The desperate few indeed
Could be helped in times of need

Senseless, dangerous and destructive
It can blow your mind
Who are these people that devastate human kind
Are they blind can they not see
That they destroy humanity
Weapons be laid to rest
A humungous test for the best
Practice gives you perfect shot

I still think heaven should not be forgot

Testing tolerance
Mass incompetence
Begging for your daily bread

This mentality eats into society
And if you aim to kill
You probably will

LOOKING THROUGH

On the dark side
Looking through
There is so much we can do
It's the feeling of one
It's begun

CHORUS:
Let it shine
Let in the good
Breathe in all the best
You can imagine
Let out fear
Let go of hate
You can leave them at the gate
On the dark side
On the dark side

On the dark side
Looking out
There's a waterfall of doubt
And it's waiting for the crossing of the line

CHORUS:
Let it shine
Let in the good
Breathe in all the best
You can imagine
Let out fear
Let go of hate
You can leave them at the gate
On the dark side

Perceptions in your brain
Return again
It's the feeling of one
It's begun

CHORUS:
Let it shine
Let in the good
Breathe in all the best
You can imagine
Let out fear
Let go of hate
You can leave them at the gate
On the dark side

Let it shine
Let in the good
Breathe in all the best you can imagine
Let out fear
Let go of hate
You can leave them at the gate

Leave fear and hate at the gate
On the dark side

13

VIP

Deep down
I'm a celebrity
Deep down
No one knows who I am
Deep down
I am available
Deep down
I am making a plan

Deep down
Noone knows anything
Deep down
My head's in a cloud
Deep down
I'm walking on halos
Deep down
I'm singing out loud

Deep down
I cannot imagine that
Deep down
You feel nothing at all
Deep down
I'm calling right out to you
Deep down
Do you get a call?

CHORUS:
This is the face I've been given
It's the one I must live in
Don't you know me?
I'm a VIP (x3)
Get to know me
I'm a VIP (x3)

Deep down
A message has impact
Deep down
Do we get through
Deep down
I'm here all alone now
Deep down
I feel something for you

Deep down
Selfish is popular
Deep down
It's sales and sell
Deep down
I'm manic and mania
Deep down I have this to tell

Deep down
I've dreams
for eternity
Deep down
I've a dream for you
Deep down
My dreams are unseen
But deep down
It don't mean they're untrue

CHORUS:
This is the face I've been given
It's the one I must live in
Don't you know me
I'm a VIP (x3)
Get to know me
I'm a VIP (x3)

BRIDGE:
This is the very best drink
That I could ever think up myself
But it came not from me
And I'm not made of junk
And I'm as confident as can be

Get to know me
I'm a VIP (x3)
Isn't everybody…
A VIP (x3)
Treat everybody like
A VIP (x3)
We're the VIP
You're a VIP
Oh! We're the VIP
The VIP

EVOLUTION

Once there was a time when there was no time
There was a place where there was nothing
And no matter around
Once there was a motion moved the ocean
Set up the sun and the moon and the stars
A natural park
Dinosaurs through to Noah's Ark

CHORUS:
And the word I heard
I'd like to share with you
You are not predominantly what you do
Though you see the sun spirituality
There is more in the vision than your mind can see

Once there was a vision called religion
It was a story based on fiction some say fallacy
Once we were united not divided
Judgements of good and of evil in our history
But what will be is written in eternity

CHORUS:
And the word I heard
I'd like to share with you
You are not predominantly what you do
Though you see the sun spirituality
There is more in the vision than your mind can see

Though we are standing still in space
We are running in a human race
And while it all comes through intentionally
We're the dancing angels of the century
But what will be is written in eternity

Go back to base start the human race
Let time take intention
Turn it to invention
Redemption repertoire
Strumming evolution on a guitar (x3)

JOBURG CITY

Going to the places
Meeting with the faces
Everywhere
Got to keep on moving
Got to keep on grooving
Got to share

This is a new beginning
We've got to keep on winning
Got to be strong
Got to get along
Got to be there

CHORUS:
Joburg city
Hub of activity
Mega, cool, awesome
And all you can imagine
Soweto to Sandton
Everything under the sun
There's something for everyone

Brothers and sisters all around the world
We are a rainbow for you all to see
We're African
This is a message for love and understanding
This message is coming from a heart of Africa
This message for love and understanding
Can be carried by each and every heart of Africa

Making friends with strangers
Looking out for dangers
Be aware
In all the luxury
There is much poverty do you care
There's fun, games and action
If you need satisfaction
Here in every place
The city soul embrace
You got to be there

CHORUS: (x2)
Joburg city
Hub of activity
Mega, cool, awesome
And all you can imagine
Soweto to Sandton
Everything under the sun
There's something for everyone

THANKS

Thanks for the sun and the moon and the stars
Thanks for the aeroplanes and fancy cars
Thanks for the TV and the radio
And the late nite special where anything goes

Thanks for the shopping centre and the mall
Thanks for everything and for one and all
Thanks for the satisfaction, want and need
Thanks for…

CHORUS:
The wish, the wonder
For the flick of the eye
For the dreams, the dreams, I pray
Thank you, I say

Thanks for the big, small and the in between
Thanks for being here, if you know what I mean
For the gratitude I want to express
Words are limited never the less

Soft and gentle thanks are due
Over time all gratitude
For every wonder holy sensed
Keep on building confidence

CHORUS:
The wish, the wonder

For the flick of the eye
For the dreams, the dreams, I pray
Thank you, I say

BRIDGE:
So take a page out of a storybook
Pay tribute now
Come a little nearer
Thank 'em lucky stars
We are gonna go far
Everyone be who you are
We are gonna raise the bar
Until it's all much clearer

Thanks for the light and the dark
A walk in the park
Thanks for the rainbow and the flowers
Thanks for the breeze and the trees and
The deep blue seas
We can go on for hours

Thank heaven and earth for
What, where, when and why
For all we may become
The power of love
All that we are made of
Thank the One above
Thanks for You and I

AFTERALL

Afterall
Do we want the same
Is it all a game
Do we win or lose
Is there really anything we choose
Or is there a masterkey
That's controlling all that we may call free choice
Do we really have a voice
Or is it just a mask
I find myself asking questions

Afterall
What is the difference between
What we say and what we mean
Is there a symbol
Is there a sign
To let us know that we are divine
Do we need evidence to change
The way we live our lives
And the way we pray
Is it coming
Is it here today

CHORUS:
Why is there the good, the bad
Why do we feel happy sad
Why are there rich, the poor
I ask is there no cure for disease
Some have it easy, some have it tough
All these questions, are they enough for The Book
I wish I could take a look at the answers

Afterall we've been through
Here's lookin' at me
Here's lookin' at you
We might have history a past line
But I swear this could be the time
Afterall is said and done
Could it be that there is one
One Creator of us all
Who started before
And ever after, will call us to task
Maybe we know and there's no need to ask

CHORUS:
Why is there the good, the bad
Why do we feel happy sad
Why are there rich, the poor
I ask is there no cure for disease
Some have it easy some have it tough
All these questions are they enough for The Book
I wish I could take a look at the answers

Why do the good die young
What do we all become
Does anyone know
Where we go when we're gone
Do we carry on
Is there something to say for the departed
Together we make history
And a memory will last
As long as there is someone to ask
To get answers

CHORUS:

19

MONEY

Money
Is it everything you want
All that you desire
Can it take you higher
Money is it all you need
Does it fill your heart with greed
I really don't know
But it is so
Money helps

CHORUS:
Money
M-O-N-E-
Why can't I be rich like them
I guess I've got to start again
Maybe this time round
The cash will be found

Money
It give you access
Nothing more
Nothing less

Money it is a tool
For playing by the rule
For thou shalt not steal
And therefore, having it is real

Money we cannot hide
Business busyness worldwide
In the lives we lead
We need money indeed

Money call for major stock control
Money alone won't make us whole
But it will provide
Fulfilment of a need inside

CHORUS:
Money
M-O-N-E
Why can't I be rich like them
I guess I've got to start again
Maybe this time round
The cash will be found

20

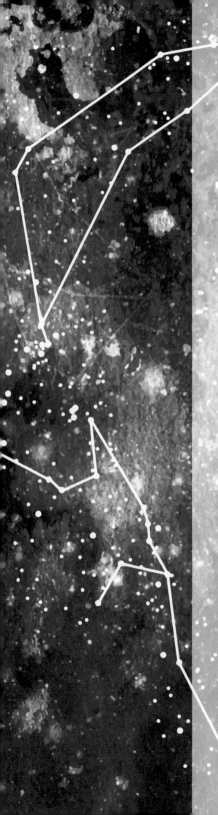

UNIVERSE

CHORUS:
Staring up at the stars
Is heaven far beyond or near
Past, present, future tenses
Purpose in the senses

Centre of the universe
Life is not a dress rehearsal

The shades of colours
Of rulers
Of people
Of class
Of better or worse
Are tipping the scales of justice

There is so much bad in the best of us
So much good in the worst of us
It hardly becomes any of us to talk about
The rest of us

Staring up at the stars

Perspective is a relative of awareness of the self
Dictatorship's irrelevant unless you're wanting help
Some will try and lift us up
Some bring us down too
Ultimate dependence on you

Shadows are productive when they help block out the sun
Sun isn't something wanted by everyone all the time

Go out of your mind into the universe

CHORUS:
Staring up at the stars
Is heaven far beyond or near
Past, present, future tenses
Purpose in the senses

Take 1
Take 1
Take 1
Come naked to the Age
Come naked to the Age
Go out of your mind into the Universe

RIDE

Ride your rainbow to a winding road
Turn to travel down a lane
Chu-chuing on a train
Flying in a plane
Run-run-running in the rain

Should we take the highway
Should we take it nice and slow
What a way to go
Should we find a passage so that we can see the light
Have you seen the light? Perhaps you might

Don't you know we can build a living dream
Do you want to lend a hand
Start the magic make it grand
Music making with the band
For peace and freedom in the land

Should we find solutions
To the questions about
If there's a doubt
We can work it out

The times are changing by the day
Keep the sunshine shining through
With a smile it's up to you
There's no time for feeling blue
Dreams of freedom have come true

Free the people from their hearts
Each person has their part to play
You know you're gonna have your say
While we learn along the way
As we're living for today

Should we stop the should we
Could we, would we,
Just decide

To take a ride

22

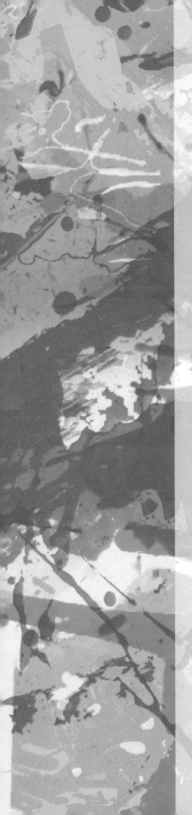

UNITE

Everyone walks around invisible
Everyone wants to be somebody special
Why do we have to be
Caught up in negativity
When we are essentially original

Everyone tries to be the best they can
Everyone wants to know the masterplan
Why do we have to be
Insensitive emotionally
When we are essentially capable

CHORUS:
People make a place
Put a smile on your face
Make the most of your days
Unite against AIDS

Everyone wants success selfishly
Everyone plays the fool occasionally
Why do we have to be
Careless with sexuality
When we are essentially spiritual

CHORUS:
People make a place
Put a smile on your face
Make the most of your days
Unite against AIDS

BRIDGE:
It's nice
But think twice
You and me
Free to be
Essentially it's nice

CHORUS: (x2)
People make a place
Put a smile on your face
Make the most of your days
Unite against AIDS

Make the most of your days
Unite against AIDS

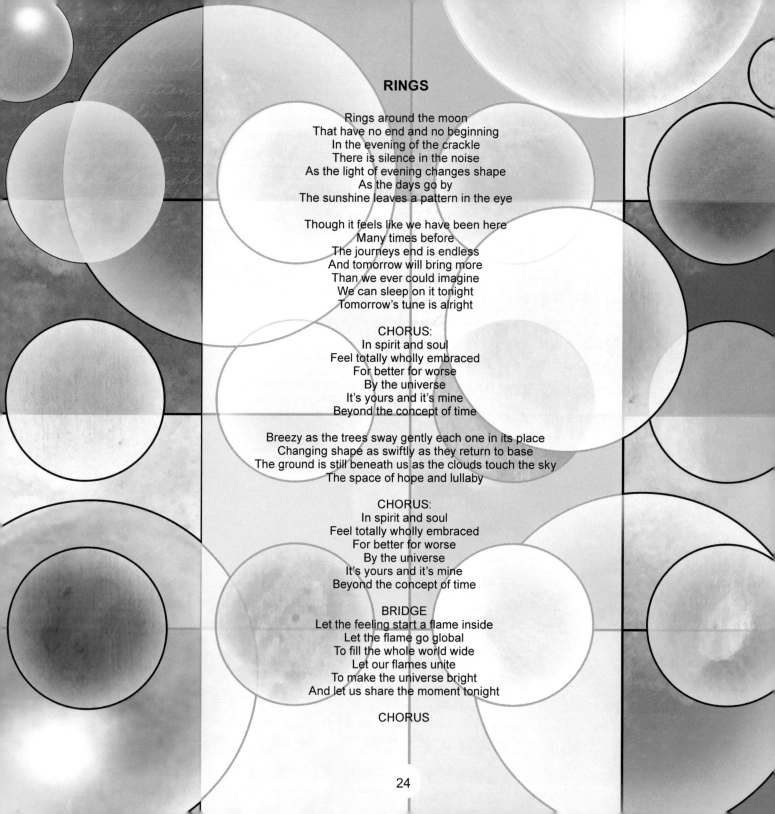

RINGS

Rings around the moon
That have no end and no beginning
In the evening of the crackle
There is silence in the noise
As the light of evening changes shape
As the days go by
The sunshine leaves a pattern in the eye

Though it feels like we have been here
Many times before
The journeys end is endless
And tomorrow will bring more
Than we ever could imagine
We can sleep on it tonight
Tomorrow's tune is alright

CHORUS:
In spirit and soul
Feel totally wholly embraced
For better for worse
By the universe
It's yours and it's mine
Beyond the concept of time

Breezy as the trees sway gently each one in its place
Changing shape as swiftly as they return to base
The ground is still beneath us as the clouds touch the sky
The space of hope and lullaby

CHORUS:
In spirit and soul
Feel totally wholly embraced
For better for worse
By the universe
It's yours and it's mine
Beyond the concept of time

BRIDGE
Let the feeling start a flame inside
Let the flame go global
To fill the whole world wide
Let our flames unite
To make the universe bright
And let us share the moment tonight

CHORUS

24

C21st

Are you getting ready for the coming of the change in guardian
Leading light from 20 centuries carry us through
Do you hold the chariot for the leading light of national dawning
Feeding through the spirit of the children at play

Lead the flame to youthful freedom
Following it's faithful footsteps forward
So we travel and we meet on the way
Go light a candle you can burn with light and lovely flicker
Fade and feel the flowers of the sun in the day

CHORUS:
Can you feel it
We're in touch
We love life so much
Stick around we're losing ground
Fearlessly flying

Shadows on the wartorn blackness
Baby born to trapped intention
We are moving quickly and the centuries okay
All we have is present moment
Use it for a celebration
Now's the time forget about yesterday

CHORUS:
Can you feel it we're in touch
We love life so much
Stick around we're losing ground
Fearlessy flying

BRIDGE:
We're coming through the ages
We've taken all the stages
We love the rock
We're on a roll
We're raving and our stories being told
Thanks for being there
It's good to know we can share
Nothing can stop us now
We're moving on

CHORUS (x2)

25

Imagination
An invitation
To love
To dream
To find meaning

A destination
A presentation
Of hope
Of faith
Of making better
We can be together
Imagine

CHORUS:
Take it up
Into the highest mountain
Let it roll across the sea
Let it be everything
Anything you want it to be

Time will tell
It will show you
How good it can be
If we imagine
Eternity

Lovely
Mystery
Momentary
Harmony
Destiny

In the silent
Touch of imagination
There is always a celebration
You can imagine
You can imagine
Imagine
Imagine

CHORUS:
Take it up
Into the highest mountain
Let it roll across the sea
Let it be everything
Anything you want it to be
Yeh

Time will tell
It will show you
How good it can be
If we imagine
Imagine
Imagine
Eternity

IMAGINATION

LOVERS

Letting go Holding onto the one
I know from then Again, you come into my mind
Every thought I'd left behind Comes back to say hello
But I'm letting go. CHORUS:
Lovers will always be lovers at heart For love is an art
It is the fire, earth, the water and air And its emotions can sail through oceans of deep
Like visions in your sleep It is desire, earth, water, air and fire.
I see your eyes I think I have paid the price
In sacrifice Love, a blessing in its time
Loving you is so divine Though what will be, will be
You will always be a part of me. CHORUS:
Lovers will always be lovers at heart For love is an art
It is the fire, earth, the water and air It's elemental
Love is the essential desire Earth, water, air and fire

MAGIC

CHORUS:
Can you imagine
In a million dreams
What kind of future tomorrow brings
Here in these times of change
We've got to rearrange the future
Give it thought, give it care
Give it magic if you dare
For it's the present that is true
So give this one to you

When we were made, we were made who we are
We could be low lives or we could be the stars
Don't ask questions that you may hide
I bet you've got the answers somewhere inside

The seeds of love are planted some place in your heart
The time to grow them is when you start
To love this life that you have got
You may choose to give your best or you may not

CHORUS

Let the magic in and you'll go far soon we'll see you as a star
I suppose that when the time is right we'll learn to love again
And if the answers we are searching for are waiting to be found
I bet we'll only find them with both feet on the ground

Choose to see the possible and recognise that fate
Well it never comes too early and I guess it don't come too late

CHORUS

LOVE IT TOGETHER

Sugar candy love machine
We are working in a team
Rainbow, music, rhythm and beat
Come to the place where the good people meet

Do we stay
Do we go
Can you tell me please
Cos I'm here
Waiting for you

This is the sign
This is the ray
This is the gift that opens my every day
This is the light
That brings in alright
And it makes everything a delicious delight

I love it together
Love it together
Love it together
Love it together

We're birds of a feather
Love it together

Like the wind
You can't see
Know
Blow
Together
Love it together
Love it together
Love it together
Love it together

Printed in the United States
By Bookmasters